Sowing In Silence

Don't Just Defy the Odds, Redefine Them

Brandon Freeman

Sowing in Silence
Don't Just Defy the Odds, Redefine Them

Author: Brandon Freeman

Published by Austin Brothers Publishing

Fort Worth, Texas

www.austinbrotherspublishing.com

ISBN 978-0-9964285-1-4

Copyright © 2015 by Brandon Freeman

Austin Brothers
Publishing

This and other books published by
Austin Brothers Publishing can be purchased at
www.austinbrotherspublishing.com

Printed in the United States of America
2015 -- First Edition

"Being alone as a child for any length of time produces fear and anxiety. But when those moments turn into hours and days, then weeks, months and years—it's pure torture!"
-Brandon Freeman

Contents

Forward

This is a book that will speak to the heart of moms, single moms, dads, single dads, grandparents–in fact to all parents that no matter how desperate your circumstances may seem, God has an answer, a plan, and a destiny for you and your family. Romans 8:28 promises us that ...*all things work together for good, for those who are called according to His purposes,* and this book speaks to young people who may feel hopeless in their circumstances of life.

Some books are written about the life of the author— stories of their childhood, background and schooling, maybe a sentence or two about hardships they have overcome, but this book takes the reader to a whole new level of survival.

Other books look at the lives of people who have overcome amazing obstacles, and they are instruction manuals for the Christian community, teaching leaders how to minister to specific groups of people.

But seldom do we find a book that tells a personal story from a child's point of view with circumstances so full of despair from the very beginning that the reader completely understands why bad choices were made, just for survival. Then that same book transcends from personal story to instruction manual on how we, in the Christian community, might recognize the symptoms of a life that has been damaged, and also teaches us how to minister the love of God to bring healing, joy, and complete redemption to life. Not that every life issue can be solved by reading this book, but it sure did remind me how even a simple act of kindness can bring that breath of fresh air to a life of empty dreams.

This is a must read for those currently experiencing tough times as they are growing up, but it also is a must read for those adults who have tried to bury their hurts from childhood and are always wondering why things never turn out the way they want.

It is a must read for those who are ministering to young adults with a past. It tells the redemptive power of God in the life of a young man from his early childhood all the way to his adulthood. In these pages you will see the hand of God at work in areas that most Christians prefer not to discuss. You will hear the heartfelt cry of this young boy trying to understand a world he was never intended to inhabit.

The pages came alive as I considered areas in life that God wants to heal, not only wants to, but is the only one with power enough to bring true healing to a life that has been so damaged by adults and life circumstances. We see how people are not the enemy a young person might think. The true enemy is Satan, working through the lives of others, and we recognize in these pages the plans he has to take us off track before we even get started. Unique's story is not just about what the Lord has done for him, but what the Lord can do for you too!

Tiz and I are so proud of Unique and the way he has used his past to frame his amazing present with the power of God!!! His story is a true miracle, and as you read these pages, you too will catch the vision of how much God loves giving us a new beginning!!! No matter who you are, where you've come from, or what you've been through, Jesus has a New Beginning for you!

Pastors Larry and Tiz Huch
DFW New Beginnings

Prologue

Growing up fatherless was the expectation of the children in my neighborhood. It wasn't unusual for a single mother to raise kids and struggle to provide food and shelter for them.

Most of my friends had this reality. Of course there was the occasional occurrence when one such mother would find her Prince Charming and she would marry. This meant the kids had a chance of growing up *normal*.

But not me...

My childhood was spent mostly in despair and shame. Hunger was my companion, and lack was my consciousness. It wasn't in any way a privileged existence for me and my sister–it was mere survival!

We wondered why life had to be this way. Lamenting our circumstances could mean not eating for that day. I quickly learned that focusing on this got in the way of getting my basic needs met. The only emotion that I felt was profitable was anger!

And I was good at it!

It was sad not having the presence of a father in my life. But to have a mother who would prefer to look for her next hit than provide stability for us was unbearable!

This book is for the person who is struggling to *get over* their childhood issues with abandonment. You are not alone anymore! I survived to tell you that you can be free too!

Jesus brought me from the depths of anguish and despair to encourage you today! Your life is worth living. The Word of God say's, *Even if my mother and father forsake me, the Lord will hold me close* (New Living Translation Psalms 27:10).

You can believe this for your life, just as I learned to believe it for mine!

Being in youth and young adult ministry today, I see a lot of youth workers grapple with how to reach young people who are struggling with everyday life. Sure there are the statistics to aide you in reaching a certain demographic. You can go to any bookstore and find some informative books on youth ministry.

There are many conferences that teach you how to equip leaders for youth and young adult ministry. Pizza night, games, and small groups are great. I assure you that it won't be enough. Many young people are suffering in silence! Just to put on clothes to go to school is a real challenge. Although abject poverty may or may not be their dilemma, their issues are real!

Be ready to sacrifice your time.

Because that is what it will take to reach those who nobody else wants to! Expect to encounter situations that will challenge you, and will at times, put the most inconvenient demand on your schedule previously thought impossible.

Welcome to a glimpse of a statistic. Prepare to ask yourself how you would reach out and minister to someone who has my experiences.

Get involved!

The school counselor should know your name. Some parents couldn't care less and some will see you as a partner in their child's success. The parents that you may or may not meet could be oblivious to the havoc they are wreaking in the lives of those who depend on them the most. Be a practical answer to prayer!

Matthew 25:35 says, *I was hungry and you gave me food to eat. I was thirsty, and you gave me drink. I was a stranger, and you took me in.* (World English Bible)

Chapter 1
I'm Alive!

"If you suffer, thank God! — it is a sure sign
that you are alive."
-Elbert Hubbard

Remembering the past is not always easy, but in order to overcome it we must face the truth it reveals. Some parts of this process are believed to be therapeutic, but in my case it just brings about a plethora of undesirable emotions. I am confident that as you and I confront our past, there is victory and peace waiting to embrace us on the other side of all the hurt and pain.

The dichotomy of the events surrounding my early years played out like a senseless drama. The days were filled with such normal events as sitting down to the table to share a meal with my family; to wondering where the next meal would come from.

My mom was a single mother of two. I never knew my father, and only remember meeting him twice when I was 7 or 8 years old. We never questioned his absence; he was nothing more than a curious visitor. We were just lucky to have our mother in our lives, doing all that she knew how to do.

It was amazing how she made life work with no help. Whether it was a simple fix or a hard task, she always found a way to make things happen. One instance that I vividly recall is a time when the water was cut off. I remember her waiting until the middle of the night to go and fill buckets at the neighbor's house, hoping not to get caught; she would heat it up so we could take a lukewarm bath.

If there was no food she would walk for miles to go to the closest food pantry to get a few things so she could make a meal. My solution was stealing food. Sometimes we would just go ask our neighbors for food. Most people were used to the occasional borrowing of sugar or something small like that. However, we were asking to borrow hot dogs, or chicken, or any unwanted items in their pantry.

When that strategy yielded no results, I would go to a friend's house and hang out for a bit. When no one was looking I would dart into the kitchen and take food. When times were desperate it wasn't uncommon for me to go to the grocery store and steal food.

I even asked the workers at a local pizzeria to give me the pizzas that they didn't use. They refused, so I would wait until no one was looking and get them from the trash. It's very embarrassing to admit this ever happened, but survival was paramount! It never occurred to me that it wasn't my responsibility to procure food for the family.

My mother never had a steady job, but when she was working she made enough money to pay rent, some bills, and put a little food on the table. Eventually we were able to get on welfare, which sometimes lightened the load.

The hard part was that we never knew which bill would go unpaid, so there were many days and nights spent with no utilities. This was the unfortunate reality that we regarded as normal.

The pain of our lifestyle was vast, but in the moment we were willing to do anything to survive.

Although at that time in my life, I was unaware of any positive effects of suffering, I now realize that my suffering brought meaning to my life in ways unknown that enabled me to keep on living. A philosopher by the name of Elbert Hubbard once said, *If you suffer. Thank God! –it is a sure sign that you are alive.*

I can face obstacles and adversity with an inner strength that was gained in my youth. I don't easily fold under pressure. I can tell myself that I've been through worse and know that it's true. It's bewildering when I think about how bad things were. We lived in a poverty stricken community, but still it always seemed like no one else had it worse than we did.

My mother never owned a car or learned to drive. Unlike the other families in our neighborhood this meant we had to walk everywhere, or scrape up enough change to ride the bus. While I really do not recall thoughts of envy, I did often wonder would we ever be in a better place in life. The difficulty was I didn't know what *better* meant.

All I knew was struggle and hardship, but could there exist outside of our reality a way of life other than this? Could there be a remote chance that somewhere on this journey there was a breakthrough waiting for me? I was tired of not being celebrated on my birthday. There is not a single memory of having a birthday party with friends and family coming over. I never sat down to a table to enjoy a slice of birthday cake even privately.

Then there was Christmas—the holiday I loved the most. This season is the one that always leaves me with so many sad memories.

I usually didn't receive gifts on my birthday or any other time from my mother as a child. One day I remember getting a lot of gifts from an organization and going to sleep joyful; until we woke up the next morning to find them all gone!

What? We were devastated!

The reality hit very hard—my mom sold everything we had gotten! She claimed that it was to pay bills, but we really had no way of verifying. That memory has haunted me for so many years. Unfortunately we were accustomed to lack being the perpetual cycle.

In school I was constantly teased by other kids for how cheap my shoes were, or how bad my clothes looked. In my own mind things were okay, but the kids at school brought it to my attention that they were not.

This was sobering and painful to me. Even the kids who lived on my block were able to get a few new things once in a while. Why not me? Why no name brand shoes or clothes? Not to mention the fact that I never knew what a washing machine looked like. All I knew was soap and water in the sink and hanging my clothes out to dry. Everything that I had to wash got washed in the sink by hand.

Though this may not be a huge deal to some, it was a big deal for me. I was always questioning my condition in life. These were questions that roamed about in my head every time I was teased. Ultimately the questions that lingered and the constant ridicule brought about terrible rage and frustration.

I needed an outlet, all of these emotions simmered until they came to a roaring boil—so I began to fight! It was a regular occurrence. Every time a kid would say something that hurt me, my anger would rise, and I would fight. With that being my mindset, this meant that I was always looking forward to a fight. It's amazing how the things that were said about me hurt so bad that it made me react in this manner. It cut me to my soul because all the things they would say were true.

I was poor, violent, misunderstood, and lonely. It was such a desperate feeling that I could not explain—who would listen? I felt like I had to prove myself tough and someone to be feared. Maybe this would be the way for me to escape being such an easy target to pick on? Maybe my reputation of being fierce would cause them to leave me alone—to suffer in silence...

Chapter 2
Absolute Silence

"Absolute silence leads to sadness. It is the image of death."
-Jean Jacques Rousseau

I grew impatient and angry with my mother; I needed answers to the questions that haunted me. I was mature past my years, and it didn't add up. Kids my age were supposed to be playing kickball and playing with action figures, not stealing food for dinner to feed the family. All of the questions of *Why* had to be answered! I began to open my eyes and look at my home situation. I had the need for it to at least make sense. I knew we were poor and it has always been like this, but why?

As I looked deeper into this maelstrom of questions, I pursued an answer. I would not be denied! You would have thought I was a private investigator. Finally, a major part of the puzzle was revealed that made our struggle clear to me. The disappointment of my discovery crushed through my soul like a wrecking ball!

The embarrassment of my findings was just one more twist in my labyrinth of despair. I couldn't believe it, but the truth had me in a choke hold, forcing me against my will to accept the results of my investigation. Nothing would be able to prepare me for the shock of my mother's crack cocaine addiction!

Even now as I think about this day, I shudder and feel nauseated.

I grew up that day.

The reality of growing up in a drug infested neighborhood finally hit home. The very thing that had molded the community into such an impoverished, dark, gloomy place of existence had found its way to my mother, and it was too late for me to do anything about it!

Can you imagine what this does to a nine year old?

What do you do?

What do you say?

How do I approach my own mother about such a thing? How do I voice to her that her actions are tearing my sister and me apart? The questions confused me; I was overcome with fear about how she would react to my discovery. Would I be able to handle the details if she were to give them to me? My system was overloaded. For now the only thing to do was be silent.

The silence was deafening but the pain spoke so loud. Only no one seemed to be listening. Inside, my mind and emotions began to grow cold. My heart was frozen in time. I became numb.

At such a young age I felt hopeless. Life didn't matter anymore. It was just a bottomless pit of lack, embarrassment, shame, and suffering. To top it off, I didn't feel like I could share this with anyone. Who would understand? Who would care about this little black boy from the ghetto?

I no longer wanted to live with this reality haunting me. Would anyone notice if I was gone? I was tired of the questions and the truth. Death became a possible answer to escaping the pain of it all. After battling those feelings for so long, thoughts of suicide filled my mind with startling frequency. The only question left was *when*?

The day started like any other. Our apartment had a rat problem, and my mom was always putting out rat poison at night. A thought came into my mind to read the small container it came in. I found out that it was just as poisonous for humans as it was for rats. Without any hesitation I put a handful of rat poison in my mouth and swallowed it all.

I waited...

All of a sudden I started to sweat profusely! My stomach hurt so bad that I could not breathe or even scream. I felt myself slipping away rapidly, and I couldn't even open my mouth to alert my mother or my sister. I was sure that I had succeeded at taking my own life!

Then out of nowhere I started vomiting uncontrollably—I couldn't stop! My mother finally heard me and rushed to my aid. She was hysterical! I had lost my will to live but the violent vomiting caused all of the poison to leave my system.

What a horrible existence. No child should have to suffer like this! I can assure you that as you read this book, there is a child contemplating their exit strategy. Sadly, many succeed.

This battle is real! There is a generation that is not reaching maturity before they have deduced that life is not worth living! You see them everywhere, they are judged, misunderstood, they may act out, they may be tatted up, or they may sit in silent indifference expecting to be overlooked, but desperately needing to be seen. They are in your community, youth group, or maybe across town in that neighborhood that you wouldn't dare drive to.

The question is what are you going to do about it?

When I look at the events that took place that day, I see the hand of God! In my lowest feeble condition His mercy allowed me to live!

Chapter 3
A new reality...all alone

"Loneliness and the feeling of being alone is the most terrible poverty."
-Mother Teresa

I remember waking up to birds chirping, a gentle breeze whistling, and the sun showing its beautiful rays across a clear blue sky. The morning felt like a dream. The smell of bacon permeated the air. My sister and I woke up and rushed to the kitchen for breakfast. The pancakes were perfectly stacked and the eggs were golden and fluffy. It was a Saturday like any other. Afterwards, it was time to do our chores, which was or routine before we could do anything else.

Once we were all finished and ready to go enjoy the day, we noticed Momma getting dressed as well. I think we both hung around a little longer just to see where she was about to go. Finally, she was dressed and ready. She came into the living room and told us that she had a few things to do, but she would be right back.

That wasn't out the norm so we never thought twice about it. Without hesitation she kissed our cheeks and went on her way. We followed outside behind her to go out and enjoy the day with our friends.

It wasn't until many hours passed and it started to get dark that we started to worry. It was already bedtime and still no sign of Momma. We didn't have a phone so there was no way we could call, or no way could she could call us. Both of us were in utter shock that it was past midnight, and we were still home alone.

We didn't sleep that night.

In that moment, we consoled each other. We figured Momma would walk through the door at any moment. So we just sat up and waited. The night gave way to morning. We saw the sun rise, yet still no sign of her. Different scenarios began to run through our heads. The feelings of fear, worry, and shock, raced without end.

I kept thinking, "Oh my God what now?"

Finally, when all the crazy thoughts and bizarre feelings settled, reality hit us both like a ton of bricks. Maybe she's not going to walk through that door like we had hoped.

My sister asked, "What will we do if she never comes back?"

I didn't know what to say or do; neither did I know how I was supposed to feel.

Something horrific kicked in as we realized that she may not be coming home after all. The reality of her crack addiction reached a level where she somehow forgot that she had children to raise. It was her deplorable obsession. We almost instinctively carried on day to day by ourselves like nothing had ever changed. It was so surreal. Neither one of us ever talked about it to other people, or to each other. Maybe we were in such a state of shock that it made us mentally and emotionally mute. It became our unspeakable secret.

I can still feel the emotions in my body when I think about it. Normal kids would go into immediate panic, or least make someone aware of what was going on—not us. It was almost as if we had rehearsed it. We did not have our mother or anyone else around, but we had each other. So we decided to live and survive on our own.

No more tears for me, because now I had to provide for my older sister. Although I was the little brother, the responsibility of being a man weighed heavily on my shoulders. Since I knew I had to do something to help us survive, I did what all the other guys around me were doing—I started to sell drugs.

Where we lived there was always an opportunity to make money. I already knew the main guy in our apartments who ran the operation. He took me under his wings and made sure that I made money. He became like a big brother to me.

I leveraged the fact that he had a crush on my sister, and often used it to my advantage. Once my sister was aware of his crush, I would make sure she came around enough so he could see her. The more he was able to see her meant the nicer he was to me, and that for me only meant more money.

After a while the money was more than enough to take care of us. At the age of twelve I was paying rent and utilities at our apartment. We always had food, and every day that was my driving force. I don't know how or why these guys chose to protect me, or give me more than I deserved. Maybe their hearts went out to me.

This was not who I dreamed of being as a little boy. I wasn't equipped to handle this way of life at my age; but I didn't spend too much time wondering about it though, it was all about self-preservation, so I had no fear. I was a nightmare running loose on the streets. I was hurt, angry, and misguided.

After a year or so, those days came to a close. I don't remember how, but a few people were made aware of the situation. I wasn't happy about it in the least bit. Maybe my sister wanted to be rescued, or wanted someone to take us in, but not me. I wanted it to just be us. I had settled in my mind that if my own mother could walk out on us, then any other situation would be hopeless.

It would be unfair of me to recant the ills of my childhood without mentioning those along the way who lifted our spirits and gave us hope of a brighter day.

My mind takes me to when I was in the third grade; a substitute teacher by the name of Mrs. Julie Young made her mark on our life. She was that black mother that you did not see in the hood—the Claire Huxtable type. She was a polished, intelligent, and highly articulate lady. She actually liked me, and was kind-hearted to me even though I was so bad!

Every time I would get into trouble and be sent to the principal's office, the principal would immediately take me to Mrs. Young's class. Mrs. Young would not sugar coat anything, she would set me straight, and that would be the end of it. I respected her honesty.

Occasionally she would actually help take care of my sister and me during those elementary years. Another teacher named Mrs. Young (who was a white lady) showed us such love. She displayed in front of us what it meant to be taken care of and treated when you are loved.

I came to school one day with my shoes busted up on the bottom. When I got to her class, I ran in to get there before all of the kids so I could duct tape my shoes together. That day in class, someone started to make fun of me for taping my shoes together, and I got into a fight. After class was over, she came to me and started crying, and took off my shoe and put it back on. I didn't know what she was doing. Later on I realized that she was looking for my shoe size.

At lunch time she went to the nearest store and bought a new pair of shoes for me! During my next period, she had me pulled out of class, and with tears in her eyes she said "one day you will be able to buy whatever shoes you want" and put the new shoes on my feet! So now I have this shoe fetish, and my closet is full of tennis shoes.

She did so much for us of her own free will. She would buy us clothes randomly, or Christmas gifts. She would make sure that we were ok without being intrusive about our home situation, and we loved her for that.

Chapter 4
Unique

*"The turning point in the process of growing up is
when you discover the core of strength
within you that survives all hurt."*
-Max Lerner

I found out through counseling, that when my mother walked out on me, it started a cycle of mistrust in motion. I never felt like people were genuine. Never felt that anybody could truly love me or want me. Of course that mindset held me captive.

My thoughts on the whole *I love you* phrase were very conflicted. Did love really exist for me on an ongoing basis? I'm talking about a love that wouldn't leave. I'm not sure people understood the magnitude of those words. I had become hardened in so many ways. I learned to resist those who expressed love out of fear. This made me very lonely.

With everything that my sister and I felt obligated to hide, the one thing that seemed to be the best outlet for me was music. Even when we struggled at home, I could always count on going to church and gleaning from the musicians. That is ultimately what drew me into the church world in the midst of what I was going through because of my insatiable connection to music.

One of my mom's friends played the organ, and we would sometimes go to church with him. The church van would come and pick us up. So going to church back then wasn't about what was really going on, but about the chance to learn more about music. So with an interest in playing drums, I just hung around those people. When I was 12 and 13 that was what overshadowed everything else. It was a positive escape from my reality.

There was a Sunday where the drummer didn't come to service. I remember being in the back of the church talking and joking around with the other kids my age, and the Pastor's wife called me out. She said "come up here and play the drums." I told her that I don't know how to play the drums. When the Senior Pastor heard me say that, he grabbed my hands and put anointing oil on my hands. He prayed for my hands and said, "go over there and play the drums." I just went over there and started playing!

Being a drummer was my dream! This led to being the guy in school always beating on the tables. When guys were free style rapping, I would be the one with the beat. When they would be battling against each other, I would be beat boxing for them. There more I would have the beat for them, the more I picked up on techniques, and I started jumping in and rapping! I would say all kinds of crazy stuff that rhymed, and people thought I was good.

What is so significant about my story during that time is that nobody was pushing me to do anything. I was just being led by God, and each person I met offered a different type of encouragement along the way. I continued to drum and rap during school lunchtimes, which led me to an amazing person who took my respect for gospel rap up another notch. His name was Aaron, but his rapping moniker was the infamous Tree Top!

At the time, nobody in my middle school could touch him! I mean he would rap against anybody at any time; it made no difference who would challenge him. When he would rap against these other dudes, he wouldn't compromise the gospel message! It was powerful!

I started getting serious about God in middle school because all of the people I came across who influenced me greatly.

Tree Top encouraged me to rap. So I built up confidence and began entering battles. My reputation got me connected in the 8th grade to some of the most popular rappers in the school. They invited me in to battles where I would be saying all kinds of crazy stuff, and they would be rapping about God. They challenged me to clean up my lyrics. This was new for me. I understood being good in a church setting, but at school too? It seemed awkward.

However, if not for their godly example in my life, I'm not sure if I would have begun the journey to total transformation! It was being connected with guys who were walking out the gospel that my life took on a different meaning.

I was still into my routine of getting into a lot of trouble. Tree Top encouraged me to get together with some guys who were a part of a group called Actors for Christ. They started inviting me different places. I had a lot of respect for these guys; there was something different about them. The main leader, whose name was Harold Badger (we called him HB), would check on us in school. After a while he started getting really involved in my life.

It became evident that HB was being a father to me. I soaked up the times with him like a sponge. I was eager to learn whatever I could from his example.

Before long, I started going to churches with them. One night we were at a youth revival. Some of the youth drama team did a skit about being disrespectful to your parents, and all of the different themes hit home for me.

It only seemed natural to answer the alter call by going up to the front, and I gave my life to the Lord. I had done it before when I was around 11 or 12, but at 15 something changed within me, it was a true surrender of my heart and my mind! My challenges didn't go away, but my curiosity heightened toward this God they challenged me to get to know.

The beckoning of God began to increase, and I realized the ordering of my steps was leading me to cross paths with people who were strategic in my life.

After some time passed, my sister and I had legal guardians. It was a couple from the church who tried to adopt us, but there was conflict between me and the dad. HB had never left my side, his leadership continued to be there, guiding me. He didn't hesitate to discipline me both physically and spiritually!

All the guys respected him for that. He was making a difference in the schools and in each of us. It was through him that I met another important person in my life, Pastor Curtis Butler. He was a machine of a man indeed! He led a group from a prominent church in Tulsa, Oklahoma. The group was called the worship warriors.

We linked arms musically, and we ministered at the evangelism outreach concerts he called Summer Slams. Anytime he would put on a production, he would put me in it. They later moved to Dallas where we continued to join forces.

I looked up to Curtis because of the life he lived on stage, but more importantly, behind closed doors. He was the real thing. A man after God's own heart!

I played drums everywhere I could, and people started asking me to play for them. I ended up playing for a choir, and that's when I met Dooney. Being exposed to his ministry, which was Holy-Hip Hop, inspired me beyond words. He was known for doing concerts and youth outreach events with some of the largest urban ministries in DFW. To top that off he was a husband and operated his own business, a barber shop. Dooney lived in private the same way that he did in public, proclaiming Jesus Christ! To me it couldn't get any better than that. I thought he was the coolest guy in the world! I looked up to him so much. I said to myself he's got it together.

He's a Christian rapper, rapping in front of all these people. Making them move and dance, all in honor of Jesus. Every chance I could, I would go by just to hang out with him, and get my hair cut. I started rapping to him, and before you know it, he took me under his wings. I took on the stage name *Unique* as I began to grow deeper in Christ. My understanding of being fearfully and wonderfully made came closer into view. I became more and more aware of the new expectations for my life as a Christian and Christian artist.

During those early years in ministry and in my faith, I was still connected to what was once so familiar in my upbringing. It was a constant struggle trying to balance who I was becoming and who I desperately needed to leave behind. I wish I can say that after I left the altar having surrendered my life to Christ, instantly all of that baggage just disappeared.

I was in a battle with myself like Paul mentions in the New Testament *Oh, what a miserable person I am! Who will free me from this life that is dominated by sin and death?* (Romans 7:24).

This was an intense time of trying to walk in this new identity, but daily I was in a serious crisis. Do I hang with some of the characters from my past? How do I handle relationships with girls when I still have needs? I wanted an off switch, but my old sin nature kept interfering. It became a situation where I was always God conscience. I played the role publically, but I couldn't figure out how living up to that same standard could be transferred to my private daily habits.

The feelings were real. My actions made me ask, *am I too bad to be saved*? I was trying to find out who God really was, who God said I was, and how He felt about me.

Again, God in His infinite wisdom answered my questions by sending me into path of an amazing man—Pastor E. Christopher Hill who we affectionately called PC. His prophetic, in your face ministry style wouldn't let me hide behind my talents as a drummer, dancer, and rapper.

PC was always on me for some reason. He was up in my face; he wouldn't let me go. With most people I could just *perform* and essentially escape behind the veil of entertainment. It was a front I had become accustomed to using if I felt people were getting too close.

But he wouldn't be fooled! He saw right through the facade, and wouldn't allow me to just get by on performance and onstage anointing. He wanted me to learn what it was to be a man. He actually made me get a job. He told me not to come back to the youth group without a job! He didn't come with judgment—he just caused me to be better.

I took the responsibility of going deeper in the Word of God for myself. I was heavily involved in the youth department, which had a membership of about 1200 youth. I ministered through dance, music, and I was involved in many other things. This church was one of the fastest growing churches in America with a membership of over 25,000 people. The Senior Pastor was without question one of the most dynamic pastors and teachers of our time!

I knew my struggle was somehow being transformed into something that was relatable to this demographic I was in. But there were still gaps in my understanding. The questions that PC would ask me, and the insight that he offered, made me think there had to be more to it than what I was experiencing.

As I began to confront myself and contrast my life to those other kids around me that seemed to be just a little more serious than I was, I enrolled in a program at the church called Basic Training. This training gave me the groundwork to lay a foundation for my faith. A powerful minister and teacher, Bonne Moon, led the classes, and the pieces began to come together. That was the spark that set me on fire to dig in this for myself.

There were many others who mentored me and became the community I relied on for many things. I was growing up now. I could no longer blame my past for my present actions. I now had to take ownership for my behavior, which was the most painful reality I could not escape. This was a battle I had not yet won!

Chapter 5
Never the Same Again

"It's difficult to make a man miserable while he feels worthy of himself and claims kindred to the great God who made him."
Abraham Lincoln

I started going to counseling sessions to make sense of the life. The counselor brought to light something very significant in my life. When my mother walked out on me, it started a cycle of mistrust in motion. I never felt like people were genuine. I never felt that anybody could love me or want me around. Of course, that mindset held me captive, and often hindered me from having healthy relationships.

My thoughts on the whole *I love you* phrase were very conflicted. Did love really exist for me? I'm talking about a love that wouldn't leave. I'm not sure people understood the magnitude of those words they used so loosely. I had become hardened in so many ways. Out of fear, I learned to resist those who expressed love. This made me a lonely person.

When I got older and started to become interested in girls, the situation worsened. I looked for love and affection in the typical places, for all of the wrong reasons. I felt like I had to have a girlfriend because that would fill the void in my heart.

Man was I wrong!

This time in my life only became more complicated and confusing due to the gaping wound in my soul. My constant need for attention and affection caused many train wrecks. The first collision that literally changed the course of my life was one of the only stations that yielded the most precious cargo—my son!

I was ministering in dance and music at a world renowned ministry. I had one of the best mentors that anyone could ask for. Life was definitely getting better.

However, grasping the thought of me being a father at only 18 years of age was too heavy to bear. During the pregnancy I was physically present, but mentally tuned out. It didn't become a reality for me until the day my son was born.

Welcome to adult life and fatherhood!

Now I had somebody that I had to take care of. I remember being in the hospital when my son was born, and looking at him through the window of the nursery. He was a bit early, and his lungs were not fully developed, and I remember crying uncontrollably. The nurses came up to me and asked if I was ok, but I just couldn't stop crying. I didn't know if I was going to be able to handle the responsibility of it all. I didn't know what I needed to do first, or what was appropriate. I was a mess! That night is when I really cried out to God.

I told Him I was scared to death, and I needed Him to show me or send someone to show me how to do this. I didn't want to fail at being a good father. It was so important to me. I did not know what it was to be a father, but I knew that I did not want my son to experience what I did—growing up fatherless.

I wish I could say the life changing birth of my son yielded lasting results, that I never looked back, and my actions were forever changed. That would not be the case for many years to come.

A boy who had been a womanizer grew up to be a man with the same curse. This behavior was perpetual, and I didn't know how to stop it. As I aged, I thought it would just disappear, but it didn't. The birth of my first son slowed me down a bit, but I was still dealing with the dysfunction of my younger years. I didn't know how to value a woman because I was so focused on what I could get out the deal. It was all about me.

I was in a twisted cycle of escaping. Suppressing the feelings of my past or my current inadequacies always seemed to work if I had a new love to blind me. The relationships were my attempt to self-medicate. I realized I never allowed myself time to heal from any hurt or turmoil.

Maybe I couldn't see it then, but now I can admit that most of my problems in relationships came from me being needy.

I was looking for a girlfriend to give me what I didn't get from my mom. Sounds crazy I know, but it's the truth. I was disappointed that I could not find satisfaction in a relationship. My mind was perverted in my understanding of love. I knew what I needed, but was unable to look beyond myself.

There was always a different girl. I was searching for something that I now know was impossible to find. That all started when I was in the 8th grade. Later on into high school it was out of control. My emotions were all over the place. I had become careless of the feelings of others, and disregarded the damage I was causing. But again, I know this was only because I was empty, and didn't know what would remedy the longing for something deeper.

I wanted so much to be in the company of a girl who would truly want me and love me and accept all of my faults. It didn't occur to me the unfair burden I was placing on these ladies. They had no way of knowing how incapable I was at conveying a genuine love for them. I didn't understand that love keeps no record of wrongs.

So I blamed them when they couldn't fulfill this impossible request to cure me. Hoping to end this bad string of brokenness, I decided to marry. Maybe this would be the antidote that would heal my broken heart. To my great disappointment, two marriages and two children later I could not get it right.

It occurred to me, altogether too late, their feelings were just as important as mine. Although my intentions were to love these women I was married to, I was unable to deliver because I misunderstood what it meant to be a husband. I was addicted to the search for a safe place to call home, yet I didn't know how to be that for someone else. I would do anything to secure this feeling, only to find it too elusive to capture.

When you begin to acknowledge that you have work to do in this area, you embark upon a journey of self-discovery. Unknowingly, we allow people to act as puppet masters, and pull the strings of our lives as they see fit.

This is only possible when you don't know your worth and you don't who and whose you are. The one who suffers if you do not realize your value is you and anyone connected to you. I have tried to hide behind a smoke screen of external distractions hoping to go unnoticed—it doesn't work. No matter how many times I relied on my entertainer persona, or the break neck pace of ministry, God would send someone in my path that would compel me to go deeper.

I have heard it said that ignorance is bliss, but honestly, ignorance is a handicap that stifles potential from ever becoming greatness. It is not until you make the conscious decision to walk down a path of self-discovery that you can begin to gather the broken pieces, and set them at the feet of the one who knows exactly how to restore things to their rightful place.

Don't make the mistake of trying to hot glue the fragments on your own—that leads to self-destruction and collateral damage in the lives of those whom you are responsible for. When we try to help God fix us, we eventually realize the efforts are incomplete. At best, we will frustrate ourselves to no end. When we allow God to reveal who we are, He illuminates areas that we didn't even realize were broken.

In His own awesome way, He introduces us to the person in the mirror, shields us from the shock of what we see, then He begins to cover us and make all things new. The restoration that God brings is without fault; He restores us to our rightful position, and redeems the time. In Joel 2:25 God tells the Israelites, *And I will restore to you the years that the locust hath eaten, the cankerworm, and the caterpillar, and the palmerworm, my great army which I sent among you.*

Although certain discoveries you realize may hurt, it is the only way to ensure full recovery. When a bone breaks, depending on where it is located, rehab is necessary. The strength returns from the focused movement over the course of time. You have to schedule time with a trained professional to teach you how to use that broken limb until the fusing and recovery time is fulfilled.

That is why it is critical to let God direct you as you take this journey. It will take time so be patient with God and yourself.

You didn't get here overnight!

A mentor is often necessary to teach you how to function as they confront the discoveries with the healing salve of God's Word. This can happen in many ways. I am not suggesting that you open yourself up to just anyone. I am also not suggesting that you have to have someone formally mentor you in order to receive your healing.

Just trust that God will send you various people who have specific assignments concerning you. It may be a ministry on TV that speaks into your life for a season or a pastor or leader at your church. Whoever it is, they will be capable of understanding where you are and pointing you in His direction.

I know that it seems like it is going to be a lot of work—and it is! But it will be rewarding, and your life depends on it! I'm sure you understand that you always have a choice. You can easily remain the same and live life as you always have; but who will that help? Aren't you tired of the masquerade? The reality is that you are dressed for an event that is over.

Those silly disguises don't fit anymore—they are hiding a person who deserves to be introduced.

You!

As long as we take matters into our own hands and hide from the world, we are misusing our purpose. God created us to be instruments of His glory, pointing others to Him as our redeemer, our faithful friend, and our Lord. He has a place for us in the Kingdom that is to come. We cannot remain ensnared in the things that happened to us in this life.

Yes, they hurt you!

Yes, you endured it!

Yes, you can move on! Stop bringing the baggage from old times to new places. Each time you do you can be sure that there won't be enough room to enjoy the newness of now.

And yes, God offers your healing, and restoration for your weary soul, but will you get rid of the baggage that is no longer relevant to where you are headed?

The Bible puts it this way. *And no one puts new wine into old wineskins. For the new wine would burst the wineskins, and the wine and the skins would both be lost.* (Mark 2:22 NLT)

There are some situations that happened in your past that you will have to acknowledge, own, learn from, and move on. If not, you remain stuck in a place that was meant to be temporary; when this happens permanent decisions can be made that will consequently affect the rest of your life.

Of course all I desired to do was move on with my life, forget all that bad stuff, and somehow erase the negative memories. That never worked for me. Reason being is there are problematic behaviors that directly connect me with some sort of dysfunction from my past. We are who life has shaped us to become. Without God that is all we will ever be. Thanks to God that in Him we are new creatures. But it doesn't negate our responsibility to put a stop to those patterns, which are within our ability to change.

Therefore if any man be in Christ, he is a new creature: old things are passed away; behold all things are become new. (2 Corinthians 5:17)

This scripture says it all, but our understanding of it has made some individuals frustrated. Allow me to help with this somewhat perplexing scripture. In Christ you are a new creature. Old things have passed away, but sometimes we still deal with the residue of our past because we aren't totally healed from it. The becoming new part of this scripture is a process that takes time.

We can be guilty of reading it and thinking in that same moment that I accept Christ into my heart all things are instantly new, perfect, and whole! So I will wake up the next day after leaving an alter call and life will be heaven on earth. My bank account will fill up to six figures, the weight that I put on will be gone, and everyone I know will love me for this newness that I now walk in.

STOP!

Let's look at this realistically. Many things will be exactly the same. In fact, the hordes of hell will be on your tail, you will lose friends, and people may not believe that you have had anything significant actually happen. The newness is spiritual and instant, but the physical has to be tested and tried, which is a process perfected in time. It is a lot like exercise—if you continue to work the muscle groups through resistance and pressure, along with a proper diet and ample water supply, you will see results!

Even in working out, there are specific techniques that you have to perform. Often a trainer can help you achieve the maximum benefit. Because of their knowledge and body (fruit) it is evident that the sweat and stress of it all produces great results.

They embody goals that have been met. It in turn encourages you to follow their advice. So it is with our walk with the Lord. Over the course of time, as we walk in the Word, a pastor or mentor (personal trainer) comes along to assist us with the techniques and equipment to lead us into a healthful lifestyle in Christ Jesus. If we take heed, results are inevitable.

Behold all things have become new even in the presence of opposing feelings In order to change your future you have to first change your mind about your past. Once you change your mind, your actions will bring you into *newness* that parallels itself to the spiritual newness you accepted when you first believed.

Although it frustrates us to no end, life is full of events that are either out of our control or not exactly what we expected. Therefore a lot of times we spend our time trying to reconcile situations. Sometimes the situations that we are attempting to reconcile are open ended—still unfolding. With our limited knowledge, this can leave us in a worsened state than when we first started to *fix* the problem.

The best advice I can offer is for us to stay in our lane. The issue of sin brings about a guiltiness that is only *fixed* when we accept the finished work of the cross into our lives. When we renounce Satan and accept Jesus, He fixes the sin problem, and we receive forgiveness. What we can do to deal with the consequences that we have to deal with is where we have the control.

We can access strength through God's Word by using the weapons designed to defeat the enemy. In 1 Corinthians chapter 10 verse 4, Paul writes *For the weapons of our warfare are not carnal, but mighty through God to the pulling down of strong holds. Casting down imaginations and every high thing that exalteth itself against the knowledge of God, and bringing into captivity every thought to the obedience of Christ; and having in a readiness to revenge all disobedience, when your obedience is fulfilled.* (KJV)

What that means is God has already given us the tools to access His strength. By using the weapons of obedience to His Word, and applying boundaries to our thought life, we can accomplish a lot! It's really good news! And there you were thinking that you had to *fix* the situation. No, it was already fixed in the spirit realm, we only had to access it and enable the principal of obedience to cause desired changes to take place. Again, we have to be patient so the results have time to mature.

Chapter 6
Change of Mind

Religion that God our Father accepts as pure and
faultless is this: to look after orphans and widows
in their distress and to keep oneself
from being polluted from the world.
James 1:27

cannot imagine what type of life I would be living had it not been for men and women who decided to take a chance and help someone who could not pay them back. They invested time and energy above the call of duty, pouring life into my aching soul. How merciful is the God who placed them in my life when it was most critical? Very merciful indeed!

I've come to realize there are entire ministries that people miss the opportunity to participate in. One such ministry is to the fatherless. That is not always obvious. This would include men and women as well as children in your church and community.

There is no stereotype of fatherless child or person. They are not always delinquent, but often the void in their heart comes out as you get to know them. Begin to take interest in those who you work with and volunteer beside. You will be surprised the difference you can make.

It takes getting to know people on a deeper than surface level. If you really want to expedite the process in finding someone to minister to, ask God to reveal someone to you and He will. I promise you won't have to look far.

People all around you are suffering from this particular epidemic. Many times we have grown up and confronted our own issues with success and forget to look around us to offer a helping hand to those within our circle of influence. Maybe it is because we are afraid of the sacrifice. Maybe we simply haven't given it any thought.

I assure you that an occasional hug and greeting is not going to be enough to help guide someone in need. Sure, it might start there, but we have to be willing to be inconvenienced and get involved. We need to be ready to step in and meet the real needs according to our ability.

Take inventory of your life, and think back on a time where someone went over and above for you. If this has never happened for you, think about how it would have helped you if someone did reach out to you in this way.

As a pastor, I come in contact with people from all walks of life, different ages, and diverse cultures. I have seen a common thread woven throughout the fabric of their stories when it relates to their situations—the need for male guidance is real!

This ministry goes beyond chronological age. There are men who may or may not have children, or their children are grown. Will the real men stand up? These are the men who know how to handle their finances, and how to relate to their wives, or they are great leaders. It is these men who need to realize there is a desperate need to step into someone's life and offer spiritual and tangible guidance. You are worth more than you know! Don't underestimate that power!

Not everyone grew up where the father was absent from the home in the physical sense. Some fathers are absent because they refuse to step up to their responsibilities. Others are absent due to a divorce or estrangement. But simply providing for the basic needs of children is not enough. Sometimes the priorities become misplaced when chasing things like the next big gig or the next big boy toy consumes our time.

Don't get me wrong, I am not bashing fathers who work hard, or in cases where the mothers are blocking your ability to spend time with your children. I am speaking to those who just haven't taken the time to go deeper in mentoring their kids. Maybe it wasn't modeled for you and you feel inadequate to provide in this way. Just be willing to try. Start fresh, and ask God to show you where and how to improve your relationship with them.

Understandably, the need for a good paying job is important, but when chasing these things replaces time with your children, adjustments will have to be made.

Being a father of four kids definitely isn't easy. However, I believe it's the best thing that has ever happened to me! I know how it feels to be an outcast, even within church settings. If you have this story also, please be encouraged! Out of my four kids, two of them were out of wedlock. I had two failed marriages that produced two children and I used to be ashamed of that too. I felt disqualified to lead because of the circumstances.

I kept it a secret as much as possible simply because I knew I would be judged, and in some cases even written off. It amazes me that when we see a person's past that is against the status quo, we have a stronger tendency to judge. What about the past that is not as evident in a person's life? Does that make it any different?

You may hear different statements from the pulpit or from peers that hold you captive to your mistakes. Once you hear such things then a very strong spirit of condemnation takes over you. You begin to cringe on the inside every time someone mentions having kids out of wedlock or being divorced. I see you in the congregation when I am ministering God's Word. I watch as your blossoming countenance slowly withers into defeat. I notice you, and my heart hurts for you. My arms so badly want to reach out to you.

I wonder does anyone else see you like I do?

These are my personal questions, especially being in ministry. I know what it's like to be alienated because of this particular situation. If you've had kids out of wedlock, or you've had a divorce, then certain religious organizations will count you out immediately.

One question we have all asked God is WHY? Your why may be different from mine, but it's the constant question we all ponder. My question has been why is it that my testimony helped so many people have hope in Christ and while it helps the congregation it hurts me. Some of you may feel as I once did. Why is my testimony effective but many pastors and Christians have used my testimony against me? To them it disqualifies me. Why are we searching for perfect people to pastor an imperfect generation?

This brings me to my next question. How do you serve God and do what He has called you to do in spite of your past failures? I'm here to encourage you, strengthen you, and to tell you that life is NOT over, and you still are called to be great! If we are honest most of us will admit that we often regret our past. We don't regret our children, but rather the circumstances in which we had them. In a perfect world it is true we would have preferred to have kids when we were married, and not a moment sooner. Or we would have preferred that our marriages healed and we didn't get a divorce.

In this situation, regret is normal. It's a natural reaction brought on by true growth. The truth is that you've evolved from that which you were. You've blossomed with knowledge and understanding and a clear view point of the future. You've been delivered from bondages that once held you. The hard part is that so many people don't see it that way.

This is also not an unusual situation. Look at the life of King David. We in the body of Christ consider him a major hero in the faith. In 1 Samuel 16:7 (NIV) God tells the prophet Samuel regarding Eliab (David's older brother) *But the Lord said to Samuel "Do not consider his appearance or his height, for I have rejected him. The Lord does not look at the things people look at. People look at the outward appearance, but the Lord looks at the heart."*

People across the world praise his life although he had moments of indiscretion that caused him public shame, and a host of consequences that pursued his bloodline long after his death. In the selection process for a King, even Samuel, whom the people feared due to his status as a prophet of God, looked at Eliab and knew that he was the next in line for the coveted position—but God!!!

Your life may not look how the elite right reverends feel it should. If they reject you for fear of what *The Board* may say, look to God! He will lead you and guide you. Your life may be basic, your mistakes highlighted, and your experiences not enough in the eyes of others. But when God steps in to *anoint* you for the task, no one can stop His selection!

It's ok if they scratch their heads. You were made for this moment! It's ok if they reject you; Jesus experienced that and still does! God has a track record of choosing the most unlikely to sow in silence yet reap publicly! Just ask Moses the murderer turned deliverer, or Saul the infamous serial killer of Christians turned Apostle for Jesus Christ!

God is not keeping track of your sins and shortcomings. Once you surrender your life to Him, accept His Son, and believe on Him, and ALL of your sins are washed away! I began to confront the default settings that I had grown accustom to as each of my children was born into this world. It was the most difficult thing I had ever done. I was trying to overcome these thoughts of inadequacy, and I had to teach myself to think big in small places.

I found that my will to thrive was often suffocated by a mindset of mediocrity. This explained why each relationship ended in failure, which kept that stinking thinking on life support. It was inevitable that the next relationship would be short-lived with that toxic mindset alive in me. Something inside of me rejected this vicious cycle of despair.

With God's help, and the mentors and believers who showed up and demonstrated walking out the convictions of their faith, I pulled the plug!

You actually have the power to feed that monster, or you can starve it to death by choosing to walk in the light of God's Word. Like anything new in our lives this will take time to practice.

Chapter 7
Decisions, Decisions

"Decisions made are like seeds sown; there will eventually be a harvest so choose wisely!"
-Brandon Freeman

Decisions are so powerful. A decision made too quickly or haphazardly can change the rest of your life! Good or bad your decisions heavily influence and shape your world. We don't always make the best decisions at the best times. It is instances like this that create an atmosphere in which wrong choices are birthed.

Do you recall the moment that has now plagued you for years? Can you remember where things went sour? I challenge you to think about that moment for a second. Now that you are in touch with the hurt and pain of things gone wrong in yesteryear, be encouraged! Yes, I said it! Be encouraged! Now that you are aware of your faults and mishaps, get a big mental shovel, scoop those heartaches up, and pile them high before the throne. Then offer them to God, and let Him use those experiences to form your ministry to others who need to know that God is able to forgive those *mistakes* and use them for His glory!

I'm living proof of His mercies being new every day! Have I been rejected? Yes! Have I made wrong choices repeatedly? Yes! But now God, in His infinite wisdom, has caused my pain to push me to the platform to fulfill my purpose!

Some people don't understand why I chose to share the intimate details of my life and suffering. This book is not for them! I chose to write this book to uplift the fatherless and the motherless! I chose to write this book so those people who are dealing with the shame of their choices will see an example of someone who society labeled.

You may have been raised like me or with both parents present in your home. You may not have had all of the things that happened in my life happen to you. You might just be struggling over one wrong decision that is threatening to expose you, or is bringing fear into your mind. I tell you today that you can have the victory over what is tormenting you! The individual who, even as an adult, finds it hard to hide from the pain of confusion and wrong choices of their past, this book is for you!

It doesn't matter how many no's you get from man—God has the final say! He wants to use your story for His glory. The Bible is filled with details of people who were not likely to be considered for great positions by any human standard. However, by obedience to God, He exalted them far beyond what they would have dreamed for themselves.

Earlier in this chapter I spoke about decisions. There is a fact that we must all recognize—we cannot escape making them. No matter how hard we try to at times, even avoidance is a decision. If you are anything like me, the more painful the memory the easier it is to avoid. The problem is that what you attempt to ignore only festers and becomes more difficult to uproot in the future.

Too often we allow our victimization to force us into silence. Shame becomes our companion, and we befriend all sorts of emotions out of habit. We adopt the behavior of defeat even when the circumstances change. This is usually done subconsciously.

The Bible offers instruction on how to be more than conquerors, but the only way this is going to happen is if we do what it says. There are four definitions for *conquer* in Webster's dictionary:

1. To gain or acquire by force of arms.
2. To overcome by force of arms.
3. To gain mastery over or win by overcoming obstacles or opposition.
4. To overcome by mental or moral power.

In Romans 8:37, Paul explicitly proclaims *No, in all these things we are more than conquerors through Him who loved us.* So the good news is that we can be equipped with the weapons that make victory possible. The spiritual weaponry we need is accessed by our decision to not lean on our own understanding. We must realize that in order to conquer we must look that pain in the face and confront it.

We are not alone, God will be right there to uncover those places we have kept in the dark. Once discovered and confronted, we will need to overcome it. But how do we do that? If my problem is rage then I have to ask myself, what exactly is it that sets me off? I have to identify my triggers and the root source of that bitterness.

For me that trigger was abandonment. So how that played out in my life was that I couldn't trust anyone for fear of them getting too close and leaving me. How I began to gain control in this area of my life was to trust God to be there for me when people disappointed me. I no longer fear abandonment. In fact I rejoice if someone leaves because I know if it were good for me they would still be in my life—I am an overcomer!

Another decision I had to make was to overcome loneliness. Being lonely led me into the arms of fulfillment. With each relationship I used to medicate the aching gap in my soul, I would create a void larger than the one I was trying to fill. So I began to confront this false sense of fulfillment and validation with the Word of God.

I began to see my Kingdom value, which left no room for the false and fleeting relationships. Being alone is a choice that no longer brings fear. I intentionally seek opportunity to spend time with the lover of my soul in quietness. The Word of God says, *There is no fear in love; but perfect love cast out fear, because he who fears has not been made perfect in love.* (NKJV 1 John 4:18)

In this season of my life, I'm chasing hard after God with my time, talents, and treasure. I've learned to wait on God to select the things He wants me to focus on. Yes, the desire to be married again is there, but I choose to take my time and develop myself. No longer do I need validation from a woman. God's Word tells me who I am and for now, I am satisfied with that.

Chapter 8
Hope Restored

"When God says that our faith is the substance of what we hope for, what we are expecting, He's giving us an open invitation with no limits and no boundaries."
-Larry Huch

Depending on your purpose, your natural father can only take you so far, and someone else has to step in and take you a further to help pull and push you into your destiny. There is hope for you if you feel that your biological parents fell off at some point. Or even if they did their best, but you still feel ill-equipped, there is your Heavenly Father who will strategically place men and women as surrogates on your path to guide you on your journey to fulfillment.

It has been a privilege to see how these men and women in my life ministered and took care of people behind the scenes. I often wondered why I was able to go under their wings, but now I see. I now have to demonstrate what they opened my eyes to see. I peered in for a purpose.

Although various institutions in my Christian walk denied me opportunity, God sent my *Samuel* to anoint and appoint me at a time in my life where I had settled. It's not that I didn't believe God anymore, I was at a place where I experienced a lot of Christian fakery, and I was disappointed.

I wasn't sure about this ministry thing although I loved God. I had a lot of people speak into my life, prophesy to me about great and mighty things that were to come, and I even had some very real breakthrough experiences. But none of this really sunk in. My personal life was still full of some things that made me doubt my calling. Little did I realize everything was about to change, and God was about to reveal Himself to me in a way that would change me forever!

How I first heard about Pastors Larry & Tiz Huch was like most people—on TV. I knew him to be another big name preacher, but I didn't know his ministry was here in the DFW area until I was at TBN for a recording with Pastor Chris Hill and Bishop Jakes. Pastor Huch was one of the speakers. I met him briefly, and was told that his church was right next door. One day months later, I received a call about a church needing a drummer, and I was pursuing a place to play, so I went for the audition.

When I arrived, he was pulling up to the church. I just came from the gym and I had a cut off shirt on, and was trying to change the time for the audition so that I could be more presentable. As I was walking up to the church, I saw him pull up, but it didn't register who he was until he asked the worship Pastor, "Who is this guy?"

Tthe Worship Pastor replied, "Oh yeah he's coming to audition for the drummer position."

Pastor Huch said "Oh, ok I think I already like him because he has tattoos." Then he said, "Man you'll fit in around here because we all have tattoos."

He lifted up his sleeve and showed me his tattoos. That experience solidified much for me. When I walked into the church, I looked up and saw his picture and realized it was Pastor Huch I was comparing tattoos with, and it came back to me who he was. That moment felt like a picture of Jesus relating to people. Pastor Huch from the start, was able to show who he was, and that felt like the acceptance of a father to me. Without ever knowing my story, my Pastor reached out to me and brought a new level of significance and acceptance in my life.

The crazy thing about it is I've interviewed at a lot of churches where I was the qualified candidate for the position. I was that guy they needed on their team, but two things stopped it. Number one was my appearance did not fit the image they wanted for their staff, and number two was my past. So I was accustomed to being constantly critiqued, distrusted, and denied. The interaction with the leadership from those other experiences laid a foundation of skepticism and fear which fed my abandonment issues.

After I was hired to play the drums, Pastors Huch & Tiz came by after the service, and made it their business to tell everyone they did a good job. One Sunday, Pastor Huch, without personally knowing me, prophesied over me and said that *the Lord was preparing me for ministry because you quit because of what you've seen some things done by those in ministry and it's changed your perspective of what ministry is.* It was so on point because what I saw from those in ministry was not what I wanted to be a part of.

Eventually an opportunity came up for a college and youth leader pastor, and this person needed to be able to develop and explain ideas. The more and more I bought into the vision and helped out, the more Pastor Huch began to reel me in. Even before I was on staff, he encouraged me and told me how he loved having me around and how he appreciated my energy. He continued to pour into me and call out the leader in me.

I finally took a staff position with the church, and Pastor Huch continued to pour into me. One day he said something I'll never forget. He didn't even know at the time that I was from a fatherless home, but his words brought healing to my heart when he said, *I don't ever want you to feel like you can't talk to me, or like you don't fit in here, I don't ever want you to feel any of those things, and if you do, I need you to*

express that to me, because me and Tiz see you as our son, you
are one of our kids, whatever you need or want to talk about
the door is open.

Ever since that day that's exactly how it's been. He shows me what it really looks like to love people, not just because he loves me, but because he loves people! I think that is why he is who he is, and the church does what we do because our Pastors are not phony—they are the real deal! They make it a point to love people who are different from them.

Pastor Huch had every reason as a pastor to make coming on staff about my past, but instead he was concerned with my future. To have a great man of God speak into your life and treat you like one of his own was transformative. The experience with New Beginnings will forever be etched in my heart. The type of people I've encountered here are what it's all about! His personal testimony of overcoming drug addiction, rage, and generational curses and being victorious was to be able to offer redemption to a guy like me!

Chapter 9
Overcoming Guilt

"God doesn't deliver, heal or save you for you! You were made to deliver the message to others just like you! You are His Hands and Feet!"
-Pastor Chris Hill

There is nothing that is capable of stealing the promises of God from your life like you are. You deny yourself the ability to overcome by choosing to be silent about what God has delivered you from. There is so much scripture to support us, but often we allow ourselves to sink in the pit of despair due to guilty feelings about things that we did. If we are not speculating about what others may think of what we did, then we fret over how they may perceive us based on what happened to us. Either action can paralyze us if we allow it.

This state of paralysis can last for a moment, a season, or an entire lifetime! I'm not saying that we should not be concerned with our actions. I'm saying that we should not allow the negative actions of our past to stop us from pursuing our purpose. The only way to insure that we move past this stationary place is to confront it head on!

Let's take a moment to define what this looks like in the life of the believer. You have known all of your life that there is something you are supposed to do that will significantly solve a problem. It may be that you wake up every day with a burden for children. You read the news on the Internet, and every article on child abuse or sex trafficking causes your heart to melt. You are struggling in your personal life to find purpose, but everything you've tried to accomplish seems like a failure. At night, or upon waking up from your sleep, you dream of starting a foundation to help these little ones escape to safety. This thought that reoccurs brings you peace and joy, BUT your reality is that you have bills beyond belief due to poor decisions. You are a single parent or college student with little or no support. Maybe you feel as though nobody is there to encourage you or help you make better choices. In private you wallow in self-pity and anger.

You are in a crock pot of guilt, and the choices you made float around you serve as reminders that feed the shame you feel. It is in this state that you need to do two things:

1. Meditate on Romans 8:1 and walk it out: *Therefore, there is no condemnation to them which walk not after the flesh, but after the Spirit.*
2. Put your faults and past sins in God's hands, and keep it moving!

It may sound simple, but it is an essential process to which you will need to pass through in order to achieve your purpose in life. In my opinion, there is no better example from the Word of God on moving past guilt and condemnation of your sins and bad choices other than the life of David. He faced a penetrating ignominy as a child by his own brothers who shunned him. Scholars debate whether David's birth to Jesse was legitimate or not, but what I want to focus on is the fact that throughout his life he was not considered the most likely to succeed. I'm sure while tending sheep in the Middle Eastern pastures he questioned his worth.

Then one fateful day, the old prophet Samuel passed over all the seemingly eligible sons of Jesse. What is so riveting about this story is that Jesse never offered David to be considered as King. Samuel had to probe him by asking, *Is there anyone else?* This tells us that even among his family members he was considered the least—there is no doubt he questioned his worth.

The story goes on to tell of how David was chosen and anointed of God for the coveted position of King. Great! That was miraculous, but his troubles didn't end there. He did great and mighty things, but he made a grave mistake that cost him the life of his first-born child, AND countless problems in his household. So let's dig deeper into his sin.

In 2 Samuel 11 the story of David and Bathsheba is recorded. In 11:2 He lusts after another man's wife, by verse four he sleeps with her, by verse five she is pregnant, and by verse six, King David creates a conspiracy to conceal his adultery with Uriah's wife. The plan fails due to Uriah being a loyal and honorable man, and King David does the unthinkable to this innocent and noble man. In chapter 11 verse 14 the order to stage Uriah's death is decreed and by verse 17 Uriah is dead!

Talk about guilt! David had every reason after that point to be miserable for the rest of his days! He blew it big time, and it was known by those who looked up to him. The shame and guilt could have taken him down beyond lifting up. Especially after God used Nathan the prophet to reveal his sin and the consequences that he would have to endure. Sure he was devastated, sure he was ashamed, and he cried out to the Lord, fasted, and mourned.

Instead of wallowing in despair after his child died, he accepted the decree from God and made the decision to worship Him in spite of the dire circumstances that he created for himself. King David went on to have another son by the name of Solomon who also became King, and was considered the wisest and most wealthy man ever to live. King David continued to reign as King of Israel, and had many other accomplishments credited to his dynasty, but the point is he didn't stop living because of past sins and failures.

We have to recognize that we have a very real enemy. Your life isn't always about you. There are many things that you go through that are for others. Abraham went through what he did, but it was because of the nations within him were to be impacted. If the enemy can get you to get off focus by guilty feelings, then the nations that are supposed to know Jesus through you will be affected.

This part of the process is where I began to see things change in my life. I can assure you that my life took a totally positive turn as I began to recognize a powerful strategy of the enemy was to keep me mentally entangled and preoccupied with my failures. However it would be a lie to say that only the enemy is capable of perpetuating this oppressive force on us. He can only oppress us with guilt if we agree. Once we do, he can step back and we do the work ourselves. But wait a minute, why do we agree?

We were there and we know what we did, and often we realize that we don't deserve the goodness of God; so we kick ourselves for the choices that we made in times past and make sorry soup!

I got over what happened to me and what I did wrong. I have come to accept the decree of the Lord over my life, and I am walking out living in the Spirit while dealing with a very real reality. I cannot change the past, suffering for what I did wrong is all a part of it, but I have hope that my mistakes will free others. I don't have time to beat myself up; I need that energy to go to war for the nations within me!

I can use my life to guide and warn people as well as encourage those who don't feel they have a way out. It makes the fight worth it and the victory worth it when you take the focus off of yourself and begin to see people blessed because of my testimony, or when my spiritual sons and daughters begin to walk out their purpose. It surprises me sometimes when they begin to experience breakthrough and gain strength in their walk with the Lord, and have powerful encounters with God.

I'm even beginning to notice my biological children becoming intrigued with what I'm doing. As they see me, they are starting to ask questions... they see that preaching is what dad does and this is who he is. They want to go after the things of God for themselves now because of what they see me doing.

When you notice the times when you don't have enough in you to fight for youself, fight for somebody else, fight for those who are connected to you. Your destiny is not all about you. Get up! It is time to build your future in Jesus' name!

Chapter 10
Faith it Until You Make it

But without faith it is impossible to please him: for he that cometh to God must believe that he is, and that he is a rewarder of them that diligently seek him.

Hebrews 11:6

remember learning in 5th grade science that your personality is comprised of two things - 10% heredity and 90% of your environment makes up who you are. I no longer blame my parents for everything that I became—the despicable me. It's my surroundings that played a major part, the decisions I made because of the pain I endured. In order to make better choices I had to know what it is that I actually wanted out of life. I give Jesus all the credit for who I am now! On my journey, I learned to trust in God. He gives me the knowledge and guides my decisions. I still make mistakes, but they don't look anything like the destruction I've had to deal with in times past.

The journey of my life is far from over. The dichotomy of victory in the face of difficulty continues to be my catalyst for the miraculous. I am in constant awe of from where God has brought me. Even though I feel overwhelmed with the behind the scenes reminders that keep me humble, I am also reminded of His grace toward me. The Bible says God will never put on you more than you can bear (1 Corinthians 10:13). That tells me two things.

1. If He put it on me, He has a purpose for it.
2. When we find ourselves in situations we really can't deal with we need to look to see if we put any of it on ourselves.

It's the things that we put on ourselves that we often cannot deal with, because that's a fight we were not supposed to fight. I wrote this book from a standpoint of encouragement. With my reality, even though I'm writing this book about my past, many people aren't aware that it is in many ways still my reality. After all of this time my mom is still a drug addict.

There are plenty of times I get calls in the middle of the night and she asks me to come pick her up from here or there. Or my uncles calling, saying she hasn't come home from the previous day and it's three in the morning. Nobody knows what to do so they call me and expect me to fix it. So despite the frustration, I have to get up in the middle of the night and go look for her, and bring her back. I cannot give up on her. People need to understand that salvation is free, but the anointing costs everything you have!!! And it is worth it!

Paul calls it a *thorn in his flesh* (2 Corinthians 12:7). For Paul, some bible scholars conclude that this was a person or evil spirit the enemy sent and God used to keep him from becoming prideful. God is capable of keeping you humble so the blessings He funnels through you will not cause you to forget who they came from. Remember, Romans 8:28 declares that all things work together for good, to them who love God and are the called according to His purpose.

Your test will become your testimony, and your mess can become your message if you allow God to work it out. There is something to be said for the people who push through their mess to obey God's call on their lives for the sake of the others.

I want to be completely open and honest about where I am right now. You may see me on big stage, or speaking at a conference, but my reality is still that I may leave the event to go find my mom cracked out in an alley somewhere, and I have to get her, get her some food and clothes, or something and make sure she is safe for the moment. Seeing her in this condition often makes me want to give up, but the nations are too important for me to stop! All I've been through is for a reason, and somebody will benefit. God will get the glory—somehow!

So many people come to church for a few hours, and that time is all they have to get their minds off of the real life circumstances they face. It is the place they go only to escape. If all we wish to do is escape then we need not go to a church. Church should be the place that we go to live in community and learn the truth from God's Word to equip us for the battle at hand.

When it comes to presenting the gospel message, I ask myself what can I do or say within that 90 to 120 minutes to impact your decision making process that will affect your life? In 2 Kings 4, a widow seeks the prophet Elisha to prevent her sons from slavery due to the family debt incurred by her late husband. He tells her to borrow vessels from her neighbors, bring them into her home, and start pouring the oil out.

Her breakthrough came through the humiliation of her ego to ask for vessels from her neighbors. To me, God is saying that when you are searching for something in your life and your need is overwhelming you, go find empty vessels to pour into, and the focus is no longer on what I need God to do. In the process of filling empty vessels, He will take care of you and all for whom you are responsible. I'm reminded that God is not slack in His promise. That keeps me in those moments where my faith is being tried, and I choose to trust and stand on His word. I'm determined to walk in what God has called me to do.

Recently my son was riding in the car with me after a service where I preached, and I heard a video clip playing. I asked what is that... it sounds like me. He acknowledged that it was me. I kept hearing it over and over and over again. To my surprise he recorded me preaching the sermon from earlier, and played it in the car on the ride home. He was like, "Man dad you're really good at this."

I asked "What makes you say I'm good?"

He said "Just to see how everyone responded and even me, I could understand what you were talking about."

A couple of weeks later when he was headed to Summer Camp, he asked for more videos to put on his phone to show his friends.

A few weeks ago he went to this camp and he's seen what I'm about, but this camp experience was a time for him to encounter what God has specifically for his life. So whether it's answering a question about praying or whatever, I just try to give it to them in a way that demystifies God.

One day he asked me how to pray and I said, "Say the things that you would say to me."

Whatever it is and no matter how crazy it sounds just talk to God. The biggest thing about prayer is not only that you talk to God, but also you create an environment where God can speak to you."

For the rest of the week at camp, he was blown away that he began to hear the voice of God. I was blown away that when he returned and called me, he couldn't even speak without crying because he had his own encounter with Jesus! He actually prophesied to me and I was like really? He said the Lord told me to pray for you, and I want to tell you that I am proud of you, and the Lord says He's proud of you too! It meant so much to me because it didn't come from me or anyone else pushing him to do it.

He sought after God and God met him in a real way! He couldn't contain it. He said this at a moment that I was doing everything I possibly could, going through trying to do right and make the right decisions, to try not to give up. It was so relevant—I just needed to hear that God sees me, and my son sees me, and they are proud of me!

I was elated because in the midst of me not even fully knowing what I was doing he was watching. I didn't grow up with a father so my perspective is distant. Being a father in real-time experience has been challenging and rewarding. For me, fatherhood consists of a lot of prayer, trusting God, and winging it the rest of the way. Mary Kay Ash of the great cosmetic empire said *fake it until you make it*, but I say **Faith it until you make it**!

I pray that while I'm learning how to be a father I can pass down the father and child connection with my kids, even in the absence of me being in the home, that will foster within them a sincere desire to develop a relationship with God for themselves. If I can accomplish that then it will all be worth it!

My entire guilt trip has been the fact I am not physically there. I don't want to be the person who says I couldn't do this or that because I no longer lived with them. But what I can do is live my life so my kids have something to look at. They can see how I live and draw strength. Each of my children means the world to me. Everything I am doing now is so they will have a better set of opportunities in life. If they can look back and see I was there, and I led them to depend on the Lord, and draw a sense of self-worth from the times we shared, then my job will be complete.

I don't care what you are going thru; when you seek after God, everything around you will be changed as soon as you come to that place. No matter how guilty you feel, just keep living and praying. To single parents, especially fathers, whether you are living with your children or not, you still have a LOT of influence. Just do all you can with the time you have.

Many fathers who give up and abandon their children, do so with overwhelming feelings of guilt. Sometimes the mother or other family members constantly remind them of their failures due to a failed relationship with the mother. Don't get me wrong; I get that, but there are nations in you! Your children need you to fight for your right to be in their life and provide not only for the physical needs, but the spiritual and emotional needs they have too!

Don't be afraid to go into that dark place where seeds are being sown in your life. Do some gardening with the

Holy Spirit, and uproot the weeds that threaten to choke the life out of your harvest. You can start right where you are. Things don't need to be perfect, and you don't have to wait until you have your dream job to make it all better. Just start in humility with the one who will never leave or forsake you! Remember this—the just live by faith!

I leave you with this prayer and my support as a fellow bondservant of our Lord Jesus Christ on your journey.

Thank you Heavenly Father for picking me up so many times. Thank you for reaching out to me when I was in despair. Thank you for cleaning my life up, and showing me true love and acceptance through your servants, and even my own children. Thank you for every person that you sent in my path to provide support in my life as a child, and even through adulthood. Let my life encourage the hands that are holding this book to seek your face for approval and strategy to help them realize their purpose that you put in them to fulfill. Please help me to be a better father than I experienced growing up, to my children both, natural and spiritual. Thank you for transforming the lives of all who will be connected to me through the sharing of my vulnerabilities on these pages. Be glorified oh God! In Jesus name Amen!

May the God of hope fill you with all joy and peace as you trust in Him, so that you may overflow with hope by the power of the Holy Spirit.

-Romans 15:13

Epilogue

I've now come to many eye opening conclusions and plenty of revitalizing revelations. My understanding has been refined and sharpened. I know that life brings me what may be my reality, but I can't afford to buy into it. I cannot afford that bill. My life has to be spent declaring God's Word over every situation, and trusting Him even when I can't trace Him. I wrote this book as a resource for single mothers by speaking from the perspective of a wayward son.

My prayer is to inspire both that wayward child and that parent who seems to never understand. Hopefully you have been encouraged and enlightened. Prayerfully, you feel as if you can go further now, and not be held back by your past or what you don't understand.

Trust in the Lord with all your heart and lean not on your own understanding; in all your ways submit to him, and he will make your paths straight.

Proverbs 3:5,6

Those words mean so much now. I no longer lean to my own understanding because my finite mind can't comprehend an infinite God. So I HAVE to trust him. Listen to your heart at this very moment. I know what it's saying. Can you hear that still small voice right now as you read? The Lord is saying, "You can do this," he's saying to you, "I've got this; I've got it all under control!!"

All we have to do is trust and walk in it. Learn freedom of speech. That means no more being silent. Talk about those things that seemingly weigh you down. Open your mouth and confess over yourself that you are free from your past, and you will make it. That's the golden ticket for your success.

Love you all with the love of God.

No More Silence

www.ingramcontent.com/pod-product-compliance
Lightning Source LLC
Chambersburg PA
CBHW062019040426
42447CB00010B/2068